LUCIA
Child of Light

*The history and traditions
of Sweden's Lucia celebration*

by Florence Ekstrand

Welcome Press

Illustrations and design by
Kris Ekstrand Molesworth.

Copyright 1989 by Florence Ekstrand.

Welcome Press

1095 "C" Street/Bay View
Mount Vernon, WA 98273

Manufactured in the U.S.A.

INTRODUCTION

It is, as Anna's king declares in the musical, a "puzzlement."

How did a black-eyed, olive-skinned maiden from sun-drenched Italy, martyred, canonized by the Holy Roman Church, become almost a patron saint of Sweden, a land where Protestant Lutheranism is the state religion? And how did December 13, the anniversary of the day St. Lucia was martyred, become one of the best-loved holidays in this Scandinavian land?

And what of the growing number of Lucia

1

Fests in this country, where girls in white robes and with crowns of blazing candles on their heads, walk down church aisles and community platforms singing in Swedish the song of the Venetian gondoliers?

Much of the story is lost in the world of myth and legend. But recorded history bears witness to many of the facts. These, blended with the myths and legends, played out against the backdrop of darkest winter, are more than anything else a paean to light: the coming of the light, light as warmth, light as promise, light as hope, light as life; light shining in the darkness.

This is the story of the Sicilian maid Lucia, her brief life and her death at 20. We follow her as she appears in Swedish legend, mingled at first with dark symbols of paganism but later the center of one of the loveliest of home traditions. It describes today's festivals in her honor and helps you, should you wish to create a festival of your own.

Our wish is that Lucia's simplicity and devotion, together with the warmth of the festival she has inspired, will be a light in your life as well.

THE LEGEND

In the year 284 a baby girl
was born to a prosperous
family of nobility in
Syracuse on the island
of Sicily. She was
christened Lucia, a name
derived from *lux*, meaning light.

Had she lived out her life as did most of the
women in this Mediterranean land, marrying,
bearing children, dying with her brood of children and grandchildren around her, we might
never have heard her name.

Instead, Lucia died a bloody death at 20, her
throat severed by the executioners sword.

For Lucia would not renounce her faith in
the new Christian religion that was spreading
from Rome to the far reaches of the empire.

3

Lucia was not one of the first martyrs; there had been many before her. But she is reputed to have been very beautiful, and she had a great devotion not only to Christ but also to the poor of her city. For this and for what must have been amazing courage, her life became a legend.

To better understand that courage, we need to look at the times into which Lucia was born. In the first years after Christ's execution, Romans saw his followers as being one and the same with the Jews. So Christians, like the Jews, were exempted from having to worship the Roman gods, a worship that represented allegiance to the Roman state.

"It is better to light one candle than to curse the darkness."

--Motto of the Christopher Society

But the growth of the movement alarmed Rome and persecution began. The executions of Peter and Paul and burning of Christians at Nero's games inaugurated a growing hostility between Christians and the empire. Nor was it always the emperors who instigated the persecution. The Roman people, suspicious of the way Christian held themselves apart, blamed every flood, famine, war and pestilence on the anger of the gods because this new breed would not worship them.

A year before Lucia was born, Diocletian was proclaimed emperor. Although he took over an empire that had been plagued by anarchy for years, those years had been good ones for the Christians. It was as if the people sought some new consolation in the midst of wars and upheavals, and the Christians grew in converts and built costly cathedrals.

> *"He was a burning and shining lamp, and you were willing to rejoice for awhile in his light."*
> *--Jesus, speaking of John the Baptist*

Diocletian had other things than religion to occupy him in the first years of his reign. The mighty empire was cracking at the seams. To better govern the vast and splintered area, Diocletian appointed Maximian, a general, as a co-ruler and set up two seats of government, himself in Nicodemia in Asia Minor and Maximian in Milan. Diocletian chose Galerius as an aide who would in time succeed him.

The new emperor established a sound currency, sold food to the poor at half price and even at no cost, initiated public works for employment, brought most of the businesses and trades under government control and set price controls on wages and goods. As might be expected, administrative costs soared and so did taxes, and soon the chief occupation of the Roman citizen was finding a way to evade taxes at any cost.

But to Galerius, the growing strength of the Christian movement posed the greatest threat to absolute rule. And when tightened restrictions brought about several scattered revolts, Diocletian agreed. In 303, the year in which Lucia was put to death, he and Maximian ordered the destruction of all Christian churches, the burning of Christian books, the dissolution of congregations, the confiscation of their property, the exclusion of Christians from public office and the punishment by death of anyone caught in a religious assembly.

Some time between the issuance of this decree in February and Diocletian's retirement in September, Lucia was put to death.

The actual details of Lucia's life, what the Church calls her *acta*, are lost in history. Although accounts of her life and the miracles connected with it are preserved in both Greek and Latin accounts, Church historians consider their sources "unhistorical."

But there are many historical proofs of her life and its impact. As early as the sixth century she was venerated in Rome among the virgin martyrs celebrated by the Church. Her name was inserted in the Canon of the Mass both in Rome and Milan. In the cemetery of St. John in Syracuse, an inscription dating from the fourth or fifth century refers to Lucia. Pope Gregory the Great indicated in a letter that Lucia was being venerated at the time. At some point she became the patron saint of Milan.

But it was the English bishop, St. Aldhelm of Sherborne, who at the end of the seventh century gave us the story of St. Lucia as we know it today. In both prose and poetry he wrote of the Sicilian maiden's life. And if the sources he used are not historically valid, certainly the story serves to justify the veneration in which she was held by the early Church.

According to St. Aldhelm, Lucia was born of noble and wealthy parents in Syracuse. Her father died when she was still an infant and her mother, Eutychia, raised her in the Christian faith. It was a faith that was the central point in Lucia's life, and at an early age she vowed to remain a virgin and to devote her life to serving Christ and the poor.

But this was a vow she told to no one and as she grew to a young woman her mother pressed her to marry a man who was not a believer. Lucia resisted. During these years her mother suffered from hemorrhaging, and Lucia persuaded her to go to the tomb of St. Agatha. Lucia accompanied her and together they offered prayers at the tomb. Eutychia was healed.

Some versions of the story say that Lucia had prayed to God that if her mother were healed she, Lucia, would never marry and would devote her life wholly to God. In any event, it was at this time that Lucia told her mother of her secret vow. She also pleaded with her mother to let her give her inheritance, which would of course have been her dowry, to the poor. Eutychia, moved and grateful for her healing, agreed.

But Lucia's suitor was furious. He had lost not only the beautiful girl who had stirred such passion in him and whom he was determined to make his own, but he had lost her handsome dowry as well. Some sources say he went to the authorities and had her declared a witch. But Aldhelm's version, more plausible in the light of the climate of those years, is that he accused her before the governor of aiding and abetting the Christians. (A story, perhaps apocryphal, has Lucia bringing food to Christians hiding in caves; because she needed both hands free to carry the food, she strapped torches to her head.)

Lucia was called before a judge and given the chance to renounce her faith. She refused. Again she was asked to recant. Again she refused. Since Lucia had already given her entire fortune to the poor, she was reduced to the fate of a woman without a dowry: she was ordered by the judge to a brothel and a life of prostitution.

But when, to the jeers and cheers of the on-lookers, soldiers came to drag her away, they could not move her. It was as if she were rooted to the spot.

"Burn her!" ordered the judge.

"The grave itself is but a covered bridge... Leading from light to light, through a brief darkness."

--Henry Wadsworth Longfellow

She was bound to a stake and a fire laid beneath her. But the fire would not light. At this point the judge called for a guard with a sword and at length the sword was thrust through her throat. Lucia of Syracuse had joined the great body of martyrs of which Stephen had been the first.

Accounts of miracles followed. Because the story had it that Lucia's eyes were gouged out before she was killed, she in time became patron saint of the blind and those with sight impairment. Sailors on the Mediterranean must have begged her help in storms - why else would gondoliers in Venice to this day sing. "Hark how the sailor's cry joyously echoes nigh, Santa Lucia, Santa Lucia!"?

But Sweden? How has she come to be almost a national symbol in a land so far removed from Sicily, so completely Protestant that Lutheranism is a state religion? Sweden, where

King Gustav Vasa and the kings who followed him during and after the Reformation ordered all statues and paintings of saints out of the churches as being too "papist?"

The story takes form as late as the 1800's, but the legends that add their color to it go all the way back to the pre-Christian era in the north.

THE CELEBRATION

Hope, like the gleaming taper's light,
Adorns and cheers our way,
And still, as darker grows the night
Emits a brighter ray.
- Oliver Goldsmith -

modern Lucia in parade

Stockholm is a sophisticated city, capitol of a highly industrialized nation. Its historic churches are for the most part sparsely attended; Stockholm is not noted for its veneration of the saints.

But in Stockholm these past years, December

produces an enthusiastic preparation and dazzling celebration of the feast day of St. Lucia of Syracuse. Sparked by one of the city's daily newspapers, businesses and residents throw themselves into selecting the year's "Lucia," who, with her white-gowned attendants and lively *stjarngossar* (star boys), will be the center of attention in a parade and ceremony in City Hall.

Part of the excitement lies in the fact that the day comes in the same week as the awarding of the Nobel Prize in Literature; the Nobel winner stays in Stockholm long enough to crown the new Lucia.

Not only Stockholm but smaller cities, towns, communities, schools, churches, businesses and organizations throughout most of Sweden mark December 13 with similar ceremonies. The story of St. Lucia is told, "Santa Lucia" is sung (usually a version that emphasizes the return of light rather than Venice's "Pure realm of harmony"), a glow of candlelight crowns the procession and *lussikatter* (saffron rolls; literally, "Lucia cats") and ginger cookies are washed down with gallons of coffee. Lucia and her attendants spend the rest of the day, often the rest of the week, visiting hospitals, nursing homes and other aged and shut-in persons.

Very early on the same morning, parents and others across the land will have awak-

ened to a knock at the bedroom door followed
by a procession of children (certainly daughters if there are any in the house) with blazing
candles, saffron buns and ginger cookies. For
the Lucia observance, that joyful obeisance to
St. Lucia and to the end of the long dark season, is above all a celebration in the home.

Marianne Forssblad, director of the Nordic
Heritage Museum in Seattle, Washington,
grew up in southern Sweden. The Santa Lucia
observance is said to have first taken hold in
this area; Marianne remembers that the day
"had such a special feeling about, so out of the
ordinary, so solemn and yet so exhilarating.

"When I was small, we'd have our own Lucia coffee in the morning and in the evening
we'd always go to my grandparents' home and
have *lussekatter* and coffee."

But it was the school observance that still
evokes memories of a day that was "more
wonderful than any of the other pre-
Christmas events.

"It was the anticipation, knowing that school
would be completely different that day; nothing would be the same. It was especially excit-
ing for girls in that eight-to-twelve-year old
age. We had our special Lucia nightgowns that
we wore all day in school.

"There we were in the morning darkness,
each of us going to school with our white
gown over our arm. They were special gowns,

always of cotton, with lace on the collar and sleeve edge. The boys had Star Boy costumes with tall pointed caps." (Actually, these were the result of melding of traditions, harking back to times when young men went from door to door on this longest night; in earliest times they simply frightened people, in later times they sang songs and begged money.)

"Our classrooms had the old-fashioned desks with an inkwell in the corner. We each got a fat candle to set in the inkwell; the candles were all lighted. The teacher read about Lucia (even the teacher was nicer on this day!). There was a small organ in each room and we sang. There was a 'main' Lucia for the school; we would hear singing down the hall and soon she would walk into our darkened room with all her attendants.

"And the smell! The smell of saffron bread and pepparkakor permeated the whole building that day! We were usually dismissed early and it was the beginning of the Christmas."

Marianne recalled that as students grew older "catching the teacher in bed" was a favorite custom.

"We'd go out about six o'clock in the morning and catch our favorite teacher in bed and bring him cookies and coffee and sing to him."

St. Lucia day in a Göteborg school: a candle in every inkwell!

Marianne agreed that the beginning of vacation may have had something to do with the festive air.

"But it was more than that. The day stood alone. I think it was the participation. Here we may go to watch a Lucia Fest, but there we wore our Lucia gowns, we lighted our candles, we sang. Whatever it was about the day, it's difficult to recapture."

How did it all begin? How did this Sicilian saint become Sweden's talisman of returning light?

Unfortunately, as in so many old traditions, the origins are lost in history.

The city observances are of recent origin, within the last 20 or 30 years. Most of the school observances began in this century. (Anders Neumueller, editor of *Swedish Press* in Vancouver, B.C., suggests that Lucia may at an earlier date have evolved from an angel in the school nativity program: the wings were eliminated and legend initiated.) Even the old home traditions from which the others have likely sprung do not seem to go back much further than the late 1700s and early 1800s.

Albert Eskerod, who so fully describes the Swedish holidays in *"Arets Fester"* ("The Year's Holidays"), believes the tradition of honoring Lucia came originally from Germany. It may have been introduced to the North by immigrant artisans and their families (*"handverkarefamiljer"*), traders and nobles.

But it may also have come earlier, when the first priests and monks from Ireland, England and southern Europe trekked through the forests of the North between the years 1000 and 1200. For they were not only evangelists and missionaries; they were storytellers, couching the gospel within dramatic tales of saints and martyrs. Surely Lucia, with her beauty, her devotion, her early martyrdom, and especially with her feast day (day of death) falling on the old Julian calendar's winter solstice - surely she must have inspired tales that were told from one generation to the next.

But the idea of the Lucia story coming from Germany is also very logical, for the old and very popular tradition of St. Nicolaus is common to both Germany and Scandinavia, dating back to the later Middle Ages.

The feast day of St. Nicolaus, December 6, was the day on which a priest or monk, dressed as the old saint and leading by a chain a figure representing the Devil, went from house to house in the parish. To good children he gave a gift, to bad children a stone.

But with the rise of Protestantism, Nicolaus fell from favor. Saints, said the followers of Luther, do not give good gifts; good gifts are from God. The emphasis of this folk tradition was then shifted to the Christchild.

But St. Nicolaus and his history of good deeds to the poor was too popular a folk figure to be banished from the homes of Germany and Holland. The figure of the chained Devil gradually disappeared but St. Nicolaus (anglicized to St. Nicholas and hybridized to Santa Claus) still lives in tradition.

There is a less likely conjecture that the Vikings, reaching southern Europe on some of their more peaceful trading missions, may have brought back stories of Christian martyrs to tell around their smoky fires; Lucia's story may have been one of them.

However it reached Sweden it became, as most traditions do, a base for local additions and embellishment. The most famous of these is the story of Lucia and the shipload of food.

At some point in history, goes the legend, Sweden was in the grip of a terrible famine. At the height of that dark, icy winter, hunger and suffering were at their worst. People were reduced to grinding tree bark to bake into a bitter bread. But on the long night of St. Lucia Day a brilliantly-lit ship came sailing across the stormy waters of Lake Vannern. At the helm stood a beautiful young woman dressed all in white, with a face so radiant that there was a glow of light all about her head. It was St. Lucia, come with a shipload of food for the hungry, all of which she distributed with a free and loving hand.

"Ah, but wait," a Sicilian would say, "that was our story first!" For in Syracuse another miracle is remembered. The people there were in the midst of great famine, and people of the city gathered in the great cathedral to implore God for help in the name of their native saint. Even as they prayed, a great ship loaded with wheat sailed into the harbor and the starving were saved. To this day when St. Lucia's Day is celebrated in Syracuse, *cuccidata,* cooked wheat, is an ingredient in all the festival foods.

Some say it was the good farmers in the big manor houses of Skane who dramatized this legend by having the eldest daughter in the house play the part of Lucia and bring coffee and food to the rest of the household on December 13. The young woman wore candles set in a crown festooned with lingonberry leaves, a custom that still persists.

> *Martyrs create faith; faith does not create martyrs.*
>
> --Miguel de Unamuno

There are records of an earlier custom in Halland, a *lan* or province also in southern Sweden. On the eve of December 13 young women carrying torches to light their way would go from one farm to the next bringing baked treats, stopping to visit a bit at each house and returning by break of day.

Eskerod sees nothing in these old folklife observances to suggest influences from the pre-Christian era. The saint's name, Lucia, is Christian in origin, derived from *lux*, (light). And Lucia herself, Eskerod stresses, is in the Christian tradition, a saint "whose glory lies in the queenly image of a crown of light."

None the less, the Lucia legend cannot help but intertwine with the many old superstitions associated with this day.

Under the Julian calendar, which was in use in Sweden until the end of the 1200s and beginning of the 1300s, the night before December 13 was the longest, darkest night of they year. It was the night when, as the saying went, "the cow from hunger bites the manger three times." In pagan times this long black night was believed to be filled with all kinds of mischief from evil spirits and creatures that came up from a nether world.

Since Sweden, along with Finland, was the last of the North countries to be Christianized, these superstitions persisted well into Christian times. (Christmas Eve, too, was a time when all the frightening spirits were said to be about.)

Because of her name, Lucia came in some circles to be associated with Lucifer, one of the Church's many names for the Devil. According to this twist of a classic folk tale, Lucia was said to have been the first wife of Adam and the mother of the *vittra* people who lived underground. (Another folk tale says the *vittra* people originated one day when God came to call on Adam and Eve. Having seen Him approaching, Eve hurriedly began to scrub her children. She had time to clean up only half of them; the others she hid. Knowing this, God declared, "That which man hides from God will God hide from man." And he banished the unwashed children to live under the earth.) Many superstitions about the *vittra* people flourished in central Sweden, home of the fäbodar, where herdswomen tended the cows in summer and where all kinds of old folk beliefs persisted.

Most of the folklore associated with his day had to do with the fact that it was the longest night and shortest day of the year. Since the Gregorian calendar, which shifted the winter solstice to December 20, has been in effect since the 1300s, one can guess how far back in history these folk beliefs go. Other folklore had to do with farming. In some parts of Sweden all threshing of grain had to be finished by St. Lucia's Day. Often the threshing would go on all night and everyone would be given food and drink when it was finished. It was also the day for butchering the Christmas pig. The butcher must be given a *lussesup* (literally, cup of light - brandy or the Christmas ale).

> *While you have the light, believe in the light, that you may become sons of light.*
>
> --St. John the Apostle

The fact that daylight in this season does not come even to southern Sweden before mid-morning led to a farmers' custom of having three breakfasts during this dark season. Even the cattle got extra fodder on this longest night as they did on Christmas Eve.

From this evolved, very likely, the custom of getting up every early on St. Lucia's Day to get a taste of *lussibit*, maybe some sweet bread and Christmas sausage. Then it became a race to see who would be first up. And then of course the last one up must have some recognition, too.

Now, here is a play on Swedish words: the last one up was a *lus*, a louse. And so the louse came into the picture: Dalsland people and also those in southeastern Norway had a saying that on Lucia night Lucia comes driving with a load of lice. (*"Lucia under Lucianatten kom körande med lusilasset."*) More play on words! And if *lusilasset* broke down, the year would be plagued with many insects. Furthermore, at this time of year, no doubt at the end of the obligatory housecleaning, one should "read out" the lice and other vermin to drive them out of the house.

How intertwined those old traditions are! Take the *lussekatter*, the twisted saffron bun that the Lucia serves to the household that morning. Are they "Lucia cats" or "light-cats?" In Germany they are still called *dovelskatt* (devil cats), harking back to the chained devil led by St. Nicolaus and to ancient beliefs that the Devil and other demons could appear in the form of cats!

So however it was that St. Lucia came into her own on this day in Sweden, the observance, like many others, has its underpinnings in ancient folklore.

And why not? Some would like to see this day a purely religious holiday, a veneration of this virgin saint and a reminder of the light of Christmas coming into the world. Others enjoy the old folklife traditions.

But the two together create a warm and joyous day. It might be considered a foretaste of Christmas but in no way should it detract from that great Christian observance. It is a simple, home-centered reminder of St. Lucia herself and a tribute to all the facets of light - the longer days, the return of the sun, the end of the dark season and, above all, a reminder of the Light of the World.

THE CONTINUATION

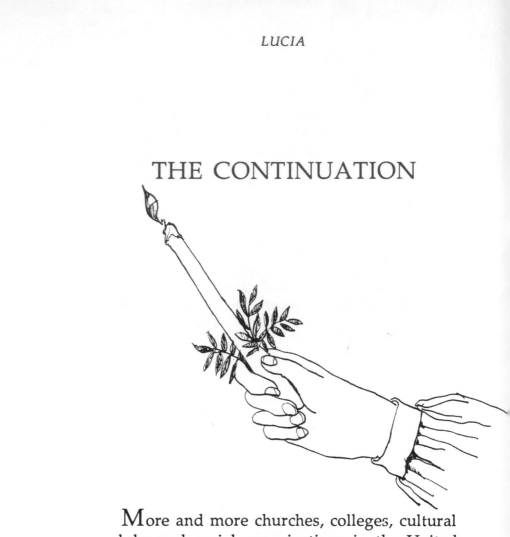

More and more churches, colleges, cultural clubs and social organizations in the United States and Canada are adopting the custom of celebrating December 13 with a Lucia Fest.

Is there anything in this tradition that would add a reverent yet festive note to your pre-Christmas weeks? Does Lucia still speak of love and sacrifice today?

Inga Marta Ahman certainly believes she does.

Born in Sweden, Inga Marta brought the tradition to her church, Our Redeemer's Lutheran in Seattle, where St. Lucia's Day had been celebrated for 20 years.

She remembers that as a child she "played" Lucia in her own home, starting at about age six.

"It wasn't observed much in northern Sweden where I grew up. But my mother was full of traditions, and we always had *Lucia Kaffe* that morning."

A celebration in a church or a community center here might be as simple as "Lucia" walking into a darkened room, her crown of candles alight, followed by white-robed attendants carrying candles and young Star Boys carrying star-tipped wands. They would sing "Santa Lucia" as they walked in, then a few Christmas carols (in the Swedish language if at all possible.) The Lucia would tell the story of the virgin martyr and her miracle on Lake Vännern.

But over the years Inga Marta has varied her programs. To make it possible for more young people to participate (children from eight years up through high school enjoy taking part), she has added "poor boys," chimney sweeps, even gingerbread boys to her procession. One year she dressed the entire Cherub

Choir as *tomter*, Christmas elves. Sometimes *"Judas med pungen"* (Judas with the money bag) dashes about as if collecting money. (In Medieval times when university stdents went from farm to farm singing and begging, one of them was dressed all in black and collected the coins; he was known as *"Judas med pungen"*).

Another time an entire family was included in the procession; they presented a basket of food to Lucia to symbolize the spirit of giving that is so much a part of the season.

"You can do as much or as little as your group can manage," says Inga Marta.

But she has strong ideas of what a Lucia Fest should not be.

It should *not* be a beauty contest. Hopefully, the girl chosen as Lucia should be able to sing, but the emphasis should be on including all the young people who are interested and who are willing to learn some Swedish songs (written out phonetically, in most cases). Swedish-speaking persons in your community can be a real help.

It should not be overdone; simple cotton gowns, a simple processional. Lucia needs no theatrics. It should involve the audience in some way, at least in some of the singing.

And of course the evening ends with everyone enjoying coffee and sweet buns and ginger cookies. There is a small tree in the social hall and while the adults are sipping coffee Inga

Marta gathers the children and they dance around the tree singing *"räven räskar över isen"* and other folk dancing songs.

Dorothy Balch remembers with delight the pre-Christmas season she and her husband Wayne spent in the home of friends in southern Sweden.

"Promptly at six o'clock on Lucia's Day we were awakened by three daughters of the family coming into our room and singing, 'Santa Lucia.' And, yes, one of them wore a crown of candles on her head and the others carried candles, and they served us saffron buns and ginger cookies.

The awarding of the Nobel Prize in literature is held December 10 in Stockhom and the winner often stays for the Lucia celebration. The story is told (we won't vouch for it) that when Sinclair Lewis was awakened at 6 a.m. by a white-clad young woman with candles blazing fom her hair, he ordered her out of the room, and hid his head under the covers!

"And since our hostess was a teacher I went with her to school and watched the children celebrate there." And the Sunday evening before, the Balches had attended a Lucia presentation at a local Covenant Church.

The experience added to the pleasure the Balches had already found in helping present a Lucia Fest in their own church. At First Covenant Church in Seattle the event has grown so large that it's been extended to two days.

Since Seattle and the surrounding area has a large Scandinavian population, this church has chosen to use the Lucia processional as the closing climax of a Swedish Advent service, with several choirs, congregational singing, Bible reading and a short meditation, most of it in Swedish.

Swedish hospitality is evident as soon as one walks into the festive entry hall filled with poinsettias, greens, red wooden horses and straw goats. Several couples extend warm greetings - in Swedish!

To Ingrid Karlsson, December 13 means helping present the big Lucia Fest of the Swedish Cultural Society in Seattle. It is the gala of the year, with an open-all-evening smorgasbord, a Lucia processional and dancing until 2 a.m. For the small children there is an early evening Lucia program a week earlier.

But Ingrid believes the Lucia tradition begins at home.

"I always bring *Lucia kaffee* to my husband in bed that morning. "No," she laughed, "I don't wear candles on my head, but we do have a special candle holder we call our Lucia candle, and I put Swedish music on the stereo and make it very festive."

Ingrid likes to invite friends over for a later coffee that morning. "And we decided that Lucias didn't all have to be young, so then *I do* wear a lighted crown when I serve my guests."

Christmas music being
played from the bell
tower of the local Luthe-
ran church invites
townspeople of Cokato,
Minnesota, to a Lucia
Coffee at 9:30 each
December 13. Candle-
light, Scandinavian
ornaments, waitresses in
costume, cardamom rolls
and Swedish mints, as
well as the Lucia herself,
greet the guests. The
custom started here in
the early 1960s, intro-
duced by Gudrun Green-
field, a daughter of the
late Dr. J.A. Aasgaard,
prominent Lutheran
clergyman.

The stately entrance hall of the American
Swedish Historical Museum in Philadelphia
provides a dramatic setting for the Museum's
Lucia ceremony on the Saturday nearest December 13. Lucia and her attendants, plus the
Star Boys, tomtes, gingerbread boys and other
small folk descend to the main stairwell and
present dances and songs. Some children begin taking part as early as age three or four.

Chairs are placed for elderly persons. "But,"

said Emily Myers, "the event is so popular that people come as much as an hour and a half early to get good standing space!"

The Museum plays host to school groups all through December. From each group a Lucia, two attendants and two Star Boys are picked. They are briefed for about 15 minutes, then they bring trays of ginger cookies to treat their classmates. The Museum also loans out Lucia crowns to schools wishing to stage their own Lucia Fest.

Two Lucia observances are scheduled each December 13 by the American Swedish Institute in Minneapolis. The early one, at seven a.m., is for Institute members and is very simple, very traditional. Members are seated in the various rooms of the charming old mansion in which the Institute is housed and are first served coffee. Then the lights go out and Lucia and her attendants form a procession from the third floor on down, stopping in each room to sing.

"This is like the home ceremony. In fact," laughed Barbro Roehrdanz, a teacher of Swedish at the Institute, "it's so simple that when it's finished some people ask, 'Is that all there is?'"

An evening celebration is open to the public in the auditorium. Here there is more singing, a children's choir, the story of Lucia. And always, Victor Rydberg's poem, *"Tomten,"* is read in both Swedish and English. Lucia and attendants are often Swedish exchange students.

The Lucia ceremony is part of a two-day *Jul Fest* at Seattle's Nordic Heritage Museum. It is presented in the auditorium as the climax to two days of crafts, foods, singing and dancing by representatives of the five Nordic groups that make up the Museum.

Early morning arrivals at Seattle-Tacoma Airport on December 13 are startled to see a Lucia and eight candle-bearing attendants going through the airport distributing saffron buns and ginger cookies to personnel at all the airlines.

"The first international flight comes in at nine, so we start early enough that we can go to Immigration and Customs and treat them before their rush begins," said Elisabeth Gurr, an employee of Scandinavian Airlines who has been arranging this special Lucia for the past three years. If there is time they explain the tradition to their colleagues.

"And to make it very authentic," she added, "our *lussekatter* and *pepparkakor* are flown in from Sweden!"

Swedes in Calgary, Alberta, always have a Lucia Fest at St. John's Lutheran Church. But last year there was a second observance when members of the Swedish Society of Calgary and the Swedish Saturday School presented

Lucia to about 100 employees of Amoco Petroleum Company in the company facility in downtown Calgary. It was part of the company's effort to promote closer ties between Amoco and the community. In return, the company contributed toward TV and video equipment to show cultural programming at the Scandinavian Center in Calgary.

TIPS FOR PLANNING YOUR LUCIA DAY

1) No Lucia observance should detract from Advent or the Christmas celebration itself. It is not a "little Christmas," nor is it a preparation for Christmas in the sense that Advent is.

Think of it as a stopping point in a busy season, a pause, a time to be glad the dark of winter will soon be changing, a time to remind yourself that the coming of Christmas is a festival of the spirit and not of the shopping mall.

As it was in early times. Lucia's day might be a deadline by which all "heavy" work (cleaning, shopping) should be done, leaving the time before Christmas free for activities with family and friends - baking, caroling, preparing food baskets, attending concerts, bringing cookies to your workplace, catching "The Messiah" and "It's a Wonderful Life" on TV, writing notes to friends.

2) Your Lucia Day celebration can be as simple as bringing coffee and cookies to your family early on the morning of December 13. Be sure you've told them the background of the day. If you have daughters, get them involved. (If you choose to carry lighted candles be sure they are firmly anchored in the candleholder and use extreme caution.)

Little boys love the Star Boy role - they are free to be somewhat more mischievous than the solemn attendants. Whether at home or in a group setting, emphasize the children's role.

Marika Sellberg Bellord, who grew up in a Stockholm apartment, remembers that the young girls in the building would organize their own Lucia celebration each year.

"We'd all be in our white gowns very early in the morning. One of the older girls would be Lucia, and we'd start at the top floor and go through each floor, knocking at doors and

singing and offering cookies. People would be waiting for us and the small children would be absolutely wide-eyed."

Marika believes it is the children who make the season magical - small attendants, their faces shining in the candlelight; children watching, candlelight mirrored in their shining eyes.

3) You might want to invite a few friends in for coffee that morning or evening, or on a Saturday morning close to the day. Be sure to bring out all your candles and candleholders for a warm, inviting setting. Tell your friends the story of Lucia, sing her song and a few light-hearted carols. The price of saffron today makes the traditional bread very expensive; why not bake your favorite coffee bread and let the ginger cookies make your peace with

tradition?

4) If you plan a Lucia Fest in your church or organization, keep it simple. No bouffant satin gowns, please! Lucia is at home in a simple cotton gown tied with a red sash; the sash may be of satin, it is perhaps symbolic of the wealth of the dowry Lucia gave to the poor.

The attendant wear gowns similar to Lucia's but tied with tinsel rope and they wear tinsel rope headbands. The Star Boys wear white shirts and dark trousers and conical hats and carry wands tipped with tinsel stars.

Purists say Lucia's crown should hold "live" candles, with extreme caution exercised. "We use a wet cloth under the crown to be sure no hot wax drips on Lucia's head," said Ingrid Karlsson, "and someone is always close by with a bucket of water." But given a crowded hall or church, not to mention your city's fire codes, a crown with battery-operated candle is much safer.

5) Since St. Lucia is revered as much for her sacrificial giving to the poor as her devotion to Christ (and surely they go hand in hand), be sure to use the festival as an occasion for sharing. Let people bring an offering for world hunger relief, canned goods for your local food bank or toys for a local charity organization.

THE SONG

"Santa Lucia, the Neapolitan Boat Song," is the day's traditional song. Many of us grew up singing it in grade school music classes, never dreaming it had anything to do with our Swedish heritage. The song is, in fact, more dedicated to the balmy night breezes of Napoli than it is to St. Lucia.

Now 'neath the silver moon
Ocean is glowing,
O'er the calm billow
Soft winds are blowing,
Here balmy breezes blow,
Pure joys invite us,
And as we gently row,
All things delight us.

Chorus:
Hark, how the sailor's cry
Joyously echoes nigh:
Santa Lucia! Santa Lucia,
Home of fair Poesy,
Realm of pure Harmony,
Santa Lucia! Santa Lucia!

When o'er thy waters
Light winds are playing,
Thy spell can soothe us,
All care allaying;

To thee, sweet Napoli,
What charms are given,
Where smiles creation,
Toil blest by heaven.

(Repeat chorus)

But many different words have been set to this sailor's song. The best known Lucia processional in Sweden has words by Arvid Rosen, written in 1928:

Natten går tunga fjät runt gård och stuva.
Kring jord, som sol'n for lät skuggorna ruva.
Då i vårt morka hus stiger med tända ljus,
Sancta Lucia, Sancta Lucia.

Natten är stor och stum. Ny hör det svingar
i alla tysta rum sus som av vingar.
Se, på vår tröskel star vitkladd, med ljus i hår
Sancta Lucia, Sancta Lucia.

"Mörkret skall flykta snart ur jordens dalar."
Så hon ett underbart ord till oss talar.
Dagen skall åter ny stiga ur rosig sky.
Sancta Lucia, Sancta Lucia.

Here it is in English, translated literally by Anne-Charlotte Harvey and used with her permission:

The night walks with heavy steps around   farm and
  cottage.
Around the earth, forsaken by the sun,
  shadows are lowering.
Then into our dark house she treads with lighted   candles,
Saint Lucia, Saint Lucia.

The night is vast and mute. Now hear
  reverberate
in all silent rooms a rustle as of wings.
See, on our threshold stands whiteclad, lights
  in her hair
Saint Lucia, Saint Lucia.

The darkness will soon take flight from the valleys of   earth.
Thus she a wonderful word to us speaks.
The day shall again, reborn, rise from a
  rosy sky.
Saint Lucia, Saint Lucia.

During part of your program you might want
to use our verses, which focus more on Lucia
and her legend.

Now in the winter night
Good folk are waiting.
See now the maid of light,
Darkness abating.
Into our hearts she walks,
Telling her story,
Candles in shining crown
Lighting her glory.

Chorus:

Symbol of love sublime,
Moving o'er space and time,
Santa Lucia, Santa Lucia.
Into this winter night,
Come, maid of shining light,
Santa Lucia, Santa Lucia.

When on this earth she walked,
Bravely confessing,
All to the poor she gave,
All felt her blessing.
Ever her legend grew,
Spanning each ocean.
Light of the longest night,
Maid of devotion.

Santa Lucia

With swinging motion

NEAPOLITAN BOAT SONG

1. Now 'neath the silver moon Ocean is glowing, O'er the calm bil - low Soft winds are blowing,
2. When o'er thy wa-ters Light winds are playing, Thy spell can soothe us, All care al-lay-ing;

Here balmy breezes blow, Pure joys in-vite us, And as we gent-ly row, All things delight us.
To thee, sweet Na-po-li, What charms are given, Where smiles cre-a - tion, Toil blest by heav-en.

Hark, how the sailor's cry Joy-ous-ly ech-oes nigh: San-ta Lu - ci - a! San-ta Lu - ci - a,

Home of fair Po-e-sy, Realm of pure Har-mo-ny, San-ta Lu - ci - a! San-ta Lu - ci - a!

This Neapolitan boat song is traditionally sung at Swedish Lucia festivals. However, the song is really about the Santa Lucia section of the city of Naples, an area named for Naples' patron saint.

THE TOMTE

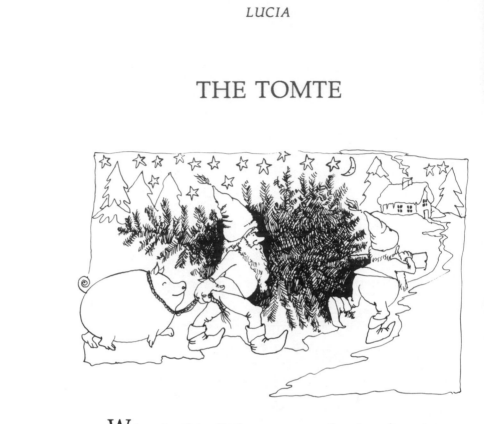

W ho is this little gnome who is often included in the Lucia processional?

The Swedish *tomte*, first cousin to the Dan-
ish and Norwegian *nisse*, has been likened to
the Irish leprechaun. But that's not quite accu-
rate, True, they're both imaginary little folk,
but while the leprechaun is found in field and
forest, the *tomte* by his very name is identified
with the home and farm: *tomt* is the Swedish
word for the site of a house - a lot or acreage.

There was a time when the *tomte* was taken
more seriously. In the 14th century St. Birgitta,

Sweden's most prolific writer of the Middle Ages, warned against *tompte gudhi*, household gods, and urged people to stop giving food to the gods on the premises.

But in later years the *tomte* has taken his place with other folk creatures as a thing of fable, a guardian of small things, friend of household pets and the cattle in the stable, stubbornly loyal to his own environs, a little slow-witted but clever in his own way. And all he asks is a bowl of rice pudding on Christmas Eve!

More than anyone else Swedish artist Jenny Nystrom gave the tomte a form. A talented classical artist in her own right, Jenny Nystrom (1854-1946) is best remembered for the thousands of charming illustrations she turned out for greeting cards of her time. At 17 she was doing magazine illustrations, and it was there she illustrated Victor Rydberg's poem, *"Tomten."* Rydberg had asked that, in keeping with the mood of his poem, the *tomte* not be portrayed as ugly as previous illustrators had made him. So Jenny used her father as a model for the *tomte's* features and patterned his body after those of old men in Lapland. She continued to draw and paint tomte figures for 70 years; it was she who first gave him a red cap. Then, little by little, her *tomter* began to be seen pulling sleds loaded with gifts.

As Anders Nuemueller has pointed out in his beautiful book on Swedish Christmas cards, *God Jul,* the Christmas card had more often created tradition than followed tradition. Today the *jultomte* holds almost the same place in Swedish Christmas traditions as Santa Claus does in ours.

As mentioned earlier, the American Swedish Institute in Minneapolis always has Rydberg's poem, *"Tomten,"* read at their Lucia Fest. We are reprinting it here, with our own translation. There is also a very lovely translation of this poem in Lorentson's book, *Of Swedish Ways.*

"TOMTEN"
by Victor Rydbery

Midvinternattens köld är hård,
stjernorna gnistra och glimma.
All sofva i ensligh gård
djupt under midnattstimma.
Manen vandrar sin tysta ban,
snön lyser hvit på fur och gran,
snön lyser hvit på taken.
Endast tomten är vaken.

Står der så grå vid ladgårdsdörr,
grå mot den hvita drifva,
tittar, som många vintrar forr,
upp emot månens skifva,
tittar mot skogen, der gran och fur
drar kring gården sin dunkla mur,

grubblar, fast ej det lär båta,
öfver en underlig gåta.

För sin hand genom skägg och hår,
skakar hufvud och hätta –
"nej, den gatan är alltför svår,
nej, jag gissar ej detta" –
slår, som han plägar, inom kort
slika sporjande tankar bort,
går att ordna och pyssla,
går att sköta sin syssla,

Går till visthus och redskapshus,
kanner på alla låsen –
korna drömma vid manens ljus
sommardrömmar i båsen;
glomsk af sele och pisk och töm
Polle i stallet har ock en dröm:
krubban han lutar öfver
fylls af doftande klöfver; –

Går till stängslet för lamm och far
ser, hur de sofva der inne;
går till hönsen, der tuppen star
stolt på sin högste pinne;
Karo i hundbots halm mar godt,
vaknar och viftar svansen smatt,
Karo sin tomte känner,
de äro gode vänner.

Tomten smyger sig sist att se
husbondsfolket det kära,
länge och val han markt, att de
hålla hans flit i ära;
barnens kammar han sen på tå
malkas att se de söta små,
ingen må det förtycka:

45

det är hans största lycka.

Så har han sett dem, far och son,
ren genom många leder
slumra som barn; men hvarifrån
kommo de väl hit neder?
Slägte följde på slägte snart,
blomstrade, åldrades,
gick - men hvart?
Gåtan, som inke låter
gissa sig, kom så åter!

Tomten vandrar till landans loft:
der har han bo och fäste
högt på skullen i höets doft
nära vid svalans näste;
nu är väl svalans boning tom,
men till våren med blad och blom
kommer hon nog tillbaka,
följd af sin näpna maka.

Då har hon alltid att qvittra om
månget ett färdeminne,
intet likväl om gatan, som
ror sig i tomtens sinne.
Genom en springa i ladans vägg
lyser månen på gubbens skägg,
strimman på skägget blänker,
tomten grubblar och tänker.

Tyst är skogen och nejden all,
lifvet der ute ar fruset,
blott från fjerran af forsens fall
höres helt sakta bruset.
Tomten lyssnar och, halft i dröm,
tycker sig höra tidens ström,
undrar, hvarthän den skall fara,

undrar, hvar källan må vara.

Midvinternattens köld är hård,
stjernorna gnistra och glimma.
Alla sofva i enslig gård
godt intill morgontimma.
Månen sänker sin tysta ban,
snön lyser hvit på fur och gran,
snön lyser hvit på taken.
Endast tomten är vaken.

THE TOMTE (The House Elf)
by Victor Rydberg

Deep in the grip of the midwinter cold
Stars send a sparkling light.
All are asleep on this lonely farm,
Deep in the winter night.
The pale white moon is wanderer,
And snow lies white on pine and fir.
Snow glows on rooftop shake.
The tomte alone is awake.

Gray, he stands by the low barn door,
Gray by the drifted snow,
Gazing, as many winters he's gazed,
Up at the moon's chill glow,
Then at the forest where fir and pine
Circle the farm in a dusky line,
Mulling relentlessly
A riddle that has no key.

Rubs his hand through his beard and hair,
Shakes his head and his cap.
"No, that question is much too deep,
I cannot fathom that."
Then making his mind up in a hurry,
He shrugs away the annoying worry;
Turns at his own command,
Turns to the task at hand.

Goes to the storehouse and toolshop doors,
Checking the locks of all,
While the cows dream on in the cold moon's light,
Summer dreams in each stall.
And free of harness and whip and rein,
Even Old Palle dreams again.
The manger he's drowsing over
Brims with fragrant clover.

The tomte *glances at sheep and lambs*
Cuddled in quiet rest.
The chickens are next, where the rooster roosts
High above straw-filled nests.
Burrowed in straw, hearty and hale,
Karo wakens and wags his tail
As if to say, "Old friend,
Partners we are to the end."

At last the tomte *tiptoes in*
To see how the housefolk fare.
He knows full well the strong esteem
They feel for his faithful care.
He tiptoes in to the children's beds,
Silently peers at their tousled heads.
There is no mistaking his pleasure:
These are his greatest treasure.

Long generations has he watched
Father to son to son
Sleeping as babes. But where, he asks,
From where, from where have they come?
Families came, families went,
Blossomed and aged, a lifetime spent,
Then - where? That riddle again
Unanswered in his brain!

Slowly he turns to the barnyard loft,
His fortress, his home and rest,
High in the mow, in the fragrant hay
Near to the swallow's nest.
The nest is empty, but in the spring
When birds mid leaves and blossoms sing,
The swallow will mark the date
And come with her tiny mate.

Then will she tales of the journey tell.
Twittering to all who hear it,
But nary a hint for the question old
That stirs in the tomte's *spirit.*
Now through cracks in the haymow wall
The moon lights tomte and hay and all,
Lights his beard through the chinks.
The tomte *ponders and thinks.*

Still is the forest and all the land,
Locked in this wintry year.
Only the distant waterfall
Whispers and sighs in his ear.
The tomte *listens and, half in dream,*
Thinks that he hears Time's endless stream,
And wonders, where is it bound?
Where is its source to be found?

Deep in the grip of the midwinter cold,
Stars send a sparkling light.
All are asleep on this lonely farm,
Late in this winter night.
The pale white moon is a wanderer,
Snow lies white on pine and fir;
Snow glows on rooftop shake.
The tomte *alone is awake.*

TRADITIONAL FOODS OF LUCIA DAY

heart-shaped cookies are served on St. Lucia day.

Sweet saffron-flavored bread made either into small buns *(luciabullar)* or into *luciakatter* (Lucia cats), the traditional curled shape, is the customary Lucia Day coffee fare, along with *pepparkakor*, ginger cookies.

The following two recipes are those taught by Inga Marta Ahman in her Swedish baking classes.

51

LUCIABULLAR or LUCIAKATTER
(Also spelled lussibullar, lussikatter)

2 cups whole milk
2 pounds all-purpose flour
2-1/2 cubes butter
1-3/4 cups sugar
3 envelopes yeast
1 cup raisins
1/2 cup chopped almonds
1 egg
2 envelopes saffron

Set aside a half cup flour for kneading the dough. Melt the butter into the milk, warming it to lukewarm. Add yeast to milk. Mix the saffron into the flour, then combine all ingredients except almonds and egg and beat well. Add flour as necessary to form a workable dough. Turn dough onto floured board and knead 10 minutes. Turn into a greased bowl, let rise until doubled in bulk. Knead again until smooth and shiny. Form into shapes or into loaves. Let rise. Brush with beaten egg, sprinkle with almonds and pearl sugar. Bake at 300 to 350 degrees, 25 to 40 minutes, depending on how dough is formed.

BOEL'S PEPPARKAKOR
(GINGER SNAPS)

*(This recipe has lots of sugar, but Inga Marta says it's one
that beginners will find easy to roll out THIN.)*

3-1/2 cups white sugar
1-3/4 cups butter or margarine
1 cup canned milk or cream
2 tablespoons cinnamon
2 tablespoons cloves
2 tablespoons ginger
2 tablespoons soda
1 cup dark Karo syrup
About 6 cups flour

Melt butter (or margarine) and cool. Add sugar, syrup and canned milk or cream. Mix flour
with spices and soda and work into liquid
mixture. Let dough rest overnight. Roll out
very thin and cut with different cookie cutters.
Bake on greased cookie sheets 5 to 7 minutes.
Watch cookies carefully.

MORMOR'S KAKOR
(GRANDMA'S COOKIES)

If you're in a hurry and haven't time to roll out cookies, here are some drop ginger cookies. They're not as sheer and crisp as the snaps, but the flavor is great.

3/4 cup margarine
3/4 cup brown sugar
1/4 cup white sugar
1 egg
2 tablespoons molasses
1-7/8 cup flour
1 teaspoon soda
1/2 teaspoon baking powder
1/2 teaspoon salt
2 teaspoons cinnamon
2 teaspoons ginger
1/2 teaspoon cloves
1 teaspoon vanilla

Beat first five ingredients. Mix dry ingredients and add all at once. Add vanilla, stir well. Drop by small teaspoonfuls on greased cookie sheet. Bake 12 to 15 minutes at 350 degrees.

Like cardamom, saffron is an exotic spice and is used in Swedish baking mainly at special occasions. How it came to be associated with Lucia fare we don't know. But perhaps because it was very special, the accompanying cookies were to be plainer fare.

None of the fancy rosettes, spritz or rich butter cookies are served now. But we're including a few of these here. For as soon as Lucia Day is past, Christmas preparations begin in earnest, and your kitchen will be as rich and aromatic as Grandma's every was!

SPRITZ COOKIES

1 lb. butter
2 cups sifted powdered sugar
2 egg yolks
3 tablespoons cream
4-1/2 cups flour
1 teaspoon almond extract

Cream butter and sugar, add egg yolks, mixing well. Add cream, flavoring, then flour and mix well. Put through cookie press on ungreased cookie sheet. Bake at 350 until very lightly browned. Cookies will "set up" once more if left on cookie sheet a few minutes after taking from oven.

BERLINER KRANSER

2 hard cooked egg yolks
1 cup sugar
1 cup butter
2 raw egg yolks
1/2 teaspoon almond or vanilla
3-1/2 cups sugar

Mash cooked yolks well. Cream butter and sugar, add both cooked and raw yolks and flavoring and mix well. Add flour and again mix well. Take about two teaspoons of dough and form a roll the thickness of a pencil. Form either into a figure 8 or a circle with ends lapped over. Dip in beaten egg white to which a few drops of cream have been added, then in sugar. Bake at 350 degrees til slightly browned. A pastry tube may be used to form a rope from which strips can be cut.

THIN KNOTS

1-3/4 cups butter
1/2 cup sugar
2 cups flour
1 egg
1 teaspoon baking powder
1/2 teaspoon almond flavoring

Using mixer, cream butter, sugar, egg and flavoring till very smooth. Stir in flour and baking powder. Chill for an hour or overnight. Roll very thin on floured board. Cut in strips (use fluted-edge pastry cutter if you have one) and form into a pretzel shape, a knot. Dip in beaten egg white which as been mixed with a few drops of cream, then dip in plain sugar or crushed loaf sugar. Bake on greased cookie sheet at 375 degrees for 10 to 12 minutes or until lightly browned..

EBE'S HAVREFLARN
(Oatmeal Lace Cookies)

1 cube butter, melted and cooled
3/4 cup sugar
1 cup oatmeal
1 tablespoon flour
1 teaspoon baking powder
1 egg

Mix all ingredients into the melted butter (can also use margarine). Grease a cookie sheet and dust flour on it. Drop on teaspoon of dough at a time; make sure they are not too close to each other. Bake at 350 degrees until golden, about 5 minutes - they brown quickly, so watch them carefully! Let cool for a second, lift off cookie with a spatula. These are a little tricky but they are good!

TO HELP YOU

A t this writing we know of no American sources for Lucia crowns that hold live candles. If you have friends or relatives in Sweden, they may be able to order them for you.

The Nordic Heritage Museum, 3014 N.W. 67th Street, Seattle, Washington 98117, sells a crown with candles powered by a very small battery that fits inside the rim of the crown. The crowns are ringed with imitation lingonberry leaves, the traditional trim. Should you wish to add more greens, twigs of small-leafed shrubs like boxwood may be used. Conifer greens (spruce, fir, etc.) are not used.

Check your local Scandinavian gift store for crowns, too, or write The Norseman Scandinavian Gifts, 30 Lakeshore Plaza, Kirkland, WA 98033.

If you have a crown holding live candles, use extreme caution. The Lucia girl's hair should be covered with two thicknesses of paper towels; some lay a sheet of foil between them. The candles (some crowns hold five, some seven; it is unclear if the number has significance) should be anchored securely in the holders. Keep a safe distance between attendants carrying candles. When smaller children are in the procession, it's wise to have adults accompany them at intervals. Unless you are prepared to use all safety measures, it is better to use battery-powered candles.

A wonderful audio cassette, "A Swedish Christmas", by Anne Charlotte Harvey with Ellen Harvey and Paul Severtson, is available from Welcome Press (see page 62). It has all the classic Lucia songs in Swedish as well as Swedish carols, Christmas hymns and traditional children's songs for dancing around the Christmas tree. It also includes a booklet giving Swedish words, English translations and a brief comment (in English) about every song on the cassette.

Also available are books that shed more light on Scandinavian holiday traditions: *Notes from a Scandinavian Parlor, Superbly Swedish, Scandinavian Christmas and* these informative coloring books: " *Swedish Cultural Coloring Book*," "*Katarzynka Color Book, Sweden*," *and* "*Christmas in Scandinavia Coloring Book*"".

Similar books about Norway, Denmark and Finland remind us that most Christmas customs vary little among the north countries.

Of much help to us in preparing this book were *"Round the Swedish Year"* by Austin and Baird (Bokfarlaget Fabel AB., Stockholm) and *"Arets Fester"* by Albert Eskerod, LT's Forlag (Stockholm). And Butler's *"Lives of the Saints"* (Christian Classics, Inc., Westminster, Maryland) gave us the historical Lucia, martyr and saint.